Advance Praise for

THE
PERSONAL DISCOVERY COURSE

& Coach Charles Shedrick

"I just completed 45 days at Malibu & I am so happy I came here. This was not my first treatment experience, but I know it will be my last. The group facilitators were great, Charles Shedrick in particular. I have said many time now that if I had worked with Charles during my first treatment, I wouldn't have had to come back. "

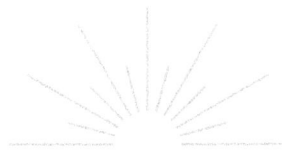

"Charles is an actual life saver. Before my husband and I came to Charles we had tried traditional therapy and couples therapy. It didn't help at all. We were on the brink of divorce when we asked Charles if he would be able to help us. We started outside of the group sessions just meeting as a couple. We found the root of our problems to be our past lives and our communication. Charles has always been a fair mediator, an excellent teacher and honest. He takes no crap and cuts right through the bs. He's intelligent but not arrogant, he's direct but not unjustifiably, and he's honest but not hurtful. My husband and I were in shambles but with Charles' help we argue less and when we do argue it's nowhere near as brutal as it was. He kept our family together and we are forever grateful he helped us do the work to stay committed."

"I have known Charles for around 15 years now and I can honestly say that I do not know where I would be today without his help. Charles is extremely knowledgeable about the 12 step process as well as other coaching modalities, but what makes Charles exceptional is his God given gift to present that information to others in a way that can be truly understood and practiced in everyday life. Charles was able to make the Big Book come alive for me, he helped me really see myself in the literature, and he helped me to feel like I truly belonged. I honestly believe that his Big Book Workshops have given me a knowledge about the process of recovery and the true nature of my disease that has saved my life.

There was a time that came when I needed to work on some of my issues outside of AA, such as the relationship with my husband and my children, and I was so fortunate to know Charles and to have him facilitate this work for me. Again, his knowledge and abilities were beyond measure, his gift of truly understanding people and the things that hold them back from growth and change is remarkable. The classes and the relationship skills workshop allowed me to learn so much about myself, about the things that affected me in my past and future, and truly allowed me to strengthen my relationships. In the last couple of years my own children have become adults and have been having their own personal struggles and I have been fortunate enough to be able to suggest the idea of meeting with Charles to them, knowing that they'll be in the best of hands! Their experience with Charles has been just as transformative as mine has and I am so excited to see what the future holds for the both of them.

It is safe to say that if you make the decision to work with Charles in any setting or method, you will be sure to find healing and learn how to make positive changes and tangible progress in your life. My entire family has had some kind of coaching with Charles and he has very literally saved our lives. Words will never be able to fully express how grateful I am to Charles and how blessed I am to have him in my life and the lives of the people that mean the most to me in this world."

THE
PERSONAL
DISCOVERY
COURSE

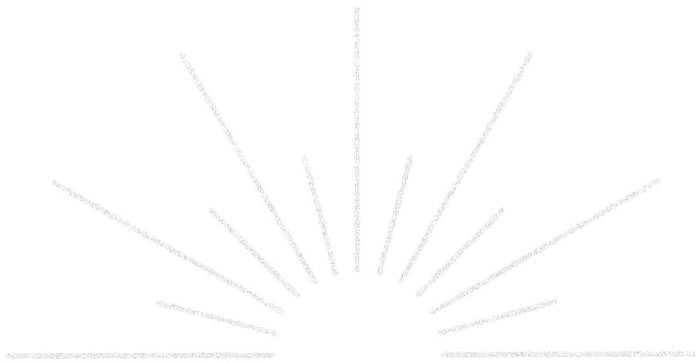

8-steps for developing genuine self-awareness,
fostering healing & enabling personal growth by
seeking to better understand the impacts of
genetic & parental influences on our lives.

CHARLES SHEDRICK COACHING

www.inomniaparatuspublishing.com

TABLE OF CONTENTS

A Note From The Author

Hi there. I'm Charles Shedrick, a Certified Life Coach & Recovery Expert. I want to congratulate you, for taking the first step towards discovering who YOU really are by picking up this workbook, and deciding to make the relationships you have, both with yourself and others, a priority. I'm honored that you've allowed me the opportunity to help you through some of the situations in life that you may be struggling with.

Something I hear from many of my clients before we begin working together is, *"Charles, I'm struggling with xyz but I don't know why, or how to stop."*

You're not alone. In this workbook, we're going to work together to identify some of the things you might be struggling with in life, as well as why those struggles even exist, and why you're holding so tightly to things that aren't serving you in any way. There's a chance that many of the beliefs you're currently fighting to maintain, aren't even yours. Think about that for a moment. Have you ever stepped back from a situation and asked yourself why you believe what you believe when you believe it? Most people don't.

For many of us, we've spent decades of our lives driving the wrong way down a one-way-freeway. Sure, we can tell that something isn't right, but we don't want to stop and ask for directions. It's easier to just keep going in the wrong direction. Or so it might seem. But not anymore. You're reached a point in life where you're tired of driving aimlessly, going nowhere. So, you've decided to pull over, and spend a little time discovering why it is you've been traveling the wrong way for so long, and figuring out what the right way is, for you and your life. It's important that throughout this process you remember that this doesn't mean you're bad, wrong, dumb, or anything like that. It simply means that you've been misinformed by misinformed people and until now, haven't taken the time to closely investigate the information you were given.

I need to tell you, this is not going to be easy. It's going to be painful, and at times, messy, but if there's no pain, there's no gain, and I will be with you every step of the way. With that, let's get started.

      – Charles Shedrick

Introduction

Each child is born perfect, whole, and complete, entering the world with infinite potential. There is no such thing as a bad child. However, every child inherits a unique genetic structure that will inform the way they develop and will determine some of the roadblocks that will influence their temperament which will in turn impact their interactions with others.

In addition to the ways, we are shaped by our genetics, we are equally impacted by the way our parents interact with us. Their capacity for healthy interactions is dependent upon their mental/physical health, their trauma, socio-economic status, culture, extended family, as well as religious training, and the education systems in which they were trained.

While we are powerless over these initial influences, understanding their impact empowers us to move beyond them, fostering healing and self-change, and that is good news. I have designed this workbook to provide a framework for your journey into self-awareness. Once you comprehend your upbringing and its impact, you gain the power to move beyond these influences.

It takes courage to begin such a journey and I want you to know how inspiring you are for taking this important step toward your liberation. As you go through this workbook bring patience and compassion to yourself. The things you will discover may be upsetting at times. You may be surprised by how challenging some of the topics are to read through. However, I urge you to stay the course. Freedom isn't free.

To become the person, you want to be you have to understand how you became the person you are. As I always say, you need to understand why you do what you do, when you do what you do.

Section 1:
Ages & Stages of Development

Childhood development involves several critical stages or ages, each characterized by significant milestones and changes in physical, cognitive, emotional, and social development. Here are some of the key stages:

Infancy (0-2 years)

- Physical Development: Rapid growth in height, weight, and motor skills. Milestones include rolling over, sitting up, crawling, and eventually walking.
- Cognitive Development: Beginnings of language development, understanding object permanence, and exploring the environment through sensory experiences.
- Emotional Development: Formation of attachments to caregivers, development of trust versus mistrust based on caregiving experiences.
- Social Development: Early interactions with caregivers and beginning to recognize and respond to social cues.

During the first stage of development, from birth to around two years old, the role of the parents/caregivers is pivotal in shaping a child's foundational understanding of the world and their emotional security. Caregivers serve as the primary source of comfort, nourishment, and stimulation for the child. Caregivers play a crucial role in forming a secure attachment bond with the child. Responsive and nurturing caregiving builds trust and a sense of security in the child, laying the groundwork for healthy relationships later in life. In addition to providing for the child's basic needs, such as feeding, changing diapers, bathing, and ensuring adequate sleep, children also require consistent and loving care that fosters a sense of safety and well-being in the child. Children also require emotional support which is provided by attentive responses to the child's cues, comforting them when distressed, and providing affection and warmth. This emotional connection promotes healthy social and emotional development.

Healthy caregivers create a stimulating environment that encourages the child to explore and learn. They engage in activities such as talking, singing, playing, and reading, which promote cognitive, language, and motor development.

Dysfunctional parenting during this early stage can have significant long-term consequences on the child's development. One potential problem that can arise from dysfunctional parenting is attachment issues. If caregivers are unresponsive, inconsistent, or neglectful, the child may develop insecure attachment patterns, leading to difficulties in forming trusting relationships later in life.

If caregivers lack emotional stability, preventing them from providing emotional support and nurturing care, it can result in emotional insecurity and instability in the child. They may struggle with regulating their emotions and forming a positive sense of self. Inadequate stimulation and neglect can impede the child's cognitive, language, and motor development, leading to developmental delays or learning difficulties. Children raised in dysfunctional environments may exhibit behavioral problems such as aggression, defiance, or withdrawal. They may struggle with self-regulation and have difficulty following rules and boundaries. Attachment Disorders: In severe cases of neglect or abuse, children may develop attachment disorders, characterized by profound difficulties in forming close relationships and trusting others. Overall, the caregiver's role during the first stage of development is fundamental in shaping the child's future well-being and functioning. Positive and nurturing caregiving fosters healthy development, while dysfunction can have lasting negative effects on the child's physical, emotional, and social development.

Early Childhood (2-6 years)

- Physical Development: Continued growth, refinement of motor skills, and increasing independence in self-care activities.
- Cognitive Development: Rapid language development, expanding vocabulary, and beginning to understand concepts such as numbers, letters, and basic cause-and-effect relationships.
- Emotional Development: Developing emotional regulation skills, increased independence from caregivers, and beginning to understand and express basic emotions.

- Social Development: Exploration of peer relationships, learning to share and take turns, as well as developing empathy and cooperation skills.

During early childhood, roughly from ages 2 to 6, caregivers continue to play a crucial role in nurturing the child's development and laying the foundation for their social, emotional, cognitive, and physical growth. Here are some key aspects of the caregiver's role during this stage. Emotional support and stability are key to providing a secure emotional base for the child, offering comfort, reassurance, and encouragement. They help the child navigate their growing range of emotions, teaching them healthy ways to express and regulate their feelings. Setting boundaries and structure by establishing consistent rules, routines, and boundaries to provide structure and predictability for the child. They guide the child's behavior with clear expectations and consequences, helping them develop self-control and respect for others. Encouraging independence fosters the child's growing sense of autonomy and independence by allowing them to make choices, solve problems, and take on age-appropriate responsibilities. They provide support and encouragement as the child explores and learns new skills. Promoting social skills by facilitating opportunities for the child to interact with peers and adults, helping them develop social skills such as sharing, cooperation, empathy, and communication. They model positive social behaviors and teach the child how to navigate social situations effectively.

Create a rich and stimulating environment that encourages the child's curiosity, creativity, and imagination. They engage in activities such as play, exploration, reading, and hands-on learning experiences that promote cognitive and language development.

Dysfunctional parenting during early childhood can have significant negative impacts on the child's development and well-being. If caregivers are inconsistent, harsh, or neglectful, the child may develop insecure attachment patterns, leading to difficulties in forming trusting relationships and regulating emotions. Children raised in chaotic or abusive environments may exhibit behavioral problems such as aggression, defiance, impulsivity, or withdrawal. They may struggle with self-regulation and have difficulty following rules and respecting boundaries. Negative or critical parenting can undermine the child's confidence and self-worth, leading to feelings of inadequacy, shame, or worthlessness. This can impact their ability to assert themselves and engage in social interactions confidently. Lack of positive role modeling and social interaction opportunities can impede the child's social development, resulting in difficulties in forming friendships, resolving conflicts, and understanding social cues.

Dysfunctional parenting may hinder the child's cognitive, language, and motor development, leading to delays or deficits in these areas.

Middle Childhood (6-12 years)

- Physical Development: Slower but steady growth, refinement of motor skills, and increased physical coordination.
- Cognitive Development: Continued language development, refinement of problem-solving skills, and increased ability to think logically and abstractly.
- Emotional Development: Developing a sense of self-identity, increased emotional independence from caregivers, and the ability to cope with more complex emotions.
- Social Development: Formation of peer groups, development of friendships, and increasing social skills such as conflict resolution and cooperation.

During early childhood, roughly from ages 6 to 12, caregivers continue to play a crucial role in supporting the child's growth and development, but the nature of their role evolves as the child becomes more independent and begins to explore the world beyond the immediate family.

Caregivers provide ongoing emotional support and guidance as the child navigates the challenges of growing up. They offer a listening ear, empathy, and encouragement, helping the child cope with stress, manage emotions, and build resilience. They encourage the child to take on increasing responsibility and independence in various aspects of their life, such as chores, homework, and decision-making. They provide guidance and supervision while allowing the child to learn from their experiences and make mistakes. Establishing clear expectations, rules, and boundaries promotes a sense of structure and safety for the child. They enforce consequences for misbehavior and teach the child about accountability and responsibility.

Children at this age need support around academics and extracurricular activities. Support includes providing assistance with homework, engaging in educational activities, and encouraging participation in extracurricular interests and hobbies. Caregivers play a key role in helping the child develop healthy habits by promoting the child's physical health and well-being by encouraging healthy eating habits, regular exercise, adequate sleep, and good hygiene practices.

Caregivers can help their children develop positive social skills and navigate peer relationships by encouraging empathy, cooperation, communication, and conflict-resolution skills. They provide opportunities for social interaction and support the child in developing meaningful friendships.

Dysfunctional parenting during early childhood (ages 6-12) can have significant negative impacts on the child's development and well-being. Negative or critical parenting can undermine the child's self-confidence and self-worth, leading to feelings of inadequacy, insecurity, or worthlessness. Children raised in chaotic, inconsistent, or abusive environments may exhibit behavioral problems such as aggression, defiance, impulsivity, or withdrawal. They may struggle with self-regulation and have difficulty following rules and respecting authority figures. Dysfunctional parenting may contribute to academic difficulties, such as poor performance in school, lack of motivation, or learning disabilities. The child may struggle to concentrate, complete assignments, or engage in classroom activities. Lack of positive social interaction opportunities and support from caregivers can lead to social isolation and difficulties forming friendships. The child may feel lonely, misunderstood, or rejected by peers. Children raised in dysfunctional environments may experience emotional instability, mood swings, or difficulty managing emotions. They may have difficulty expressing themselves or understanding the emotions of others.

Adolescence (12-18 years)

- Physical Development: Puberty and rapid physical changes including growth spurts, sexual maturation, and brain development.
- Cognitive Development: Continued refinement of abstract thinking, increased ability to consider multiple perspectives, and development of future-oriented thinking.
- Emotional Development: Exploration of identity, increased independence from caregivers, and fluctuations in mood and self-esteem.
- Social Development: Formation of more intimate peer relationships, exploration of romantic relationships, and increasing autonomy from family.

During early adolescence, roughly from ages 12 to 18, caregivers continue to play a critical role in supporting the child's growth and development, although the dynamics of their relationship may shift as the adolescent seeks greater independence and autonomy.

Caregivers provide ongoing emotional support and guidance as the adolescent navigates the challenges of adolescence, including hormonal changes, peer pressure, identity formation, and increased academic and social demands. They offer a listening ear, empathy, and encouragement, helping the adolescent cope with stress, manage emotions, and build resilience. They encourage the adolescent to take on increasing responsibility for their actions and decisions, both at home and in the wider world. They provide opportunities for the adolescent to practice independence, make choices, and learn from their experiences while offering guidance and support as needed.

Caregivers maintain clear boundaries, rules, and expectations to promote a sense of structure and safety for the adolescent. They enforce consequences for misbehavior and teach the adolescent about accountability, responsibility, and respect for others. Caregivers continue to support the adolescent's academic and career aspirations by providing guidance, encouragement, and practical assistance. They help the adolescent explore potential career paths, set educational goals, and navigate the college application process or vocational training opportunities. They promote healthy habits and self-care by encouraging healthy lifestyle habits, such as nutritious eating, regular exercise, adequate sleep, and stress management techniques. They also teach the adolescent about self-care practices and how to prioritize their own well-being.

Caregivers support the adolescent in developing healthy relationships with peers, family members, and other adults. They provide guidance on communication skills, conflict resolution, and boundaries in relationships, while also modeling positive relationship behaviors themselves.

Dysfunctional parenting during early adolescence (ages 12-18) can have significant negative impacts on the adolescent's development and well-being. Negative or critical parenting can undermine the adolescent's self-esteem and self-confidence, leading to feelings of inadequacy, insecurity, or worthlessness. This can impact their ability to assert themselves, set boundaries, and pursue their goals.

Adolescents raised in chaotic, inconsistent, or abusive environments may exhibit behavioral problems such as aggression, defiance, impulsivity, or substance abuse. They may struggle with self-regulation and have difficulty following rules and respecting authority figures. Dysfunctional parenting may contribute to academic difficulties, such as poor performance in school, lack of motivation, or truancy.

The adolescent may struggle to concentrate, complete assignments, or engage in classroom activities due to stress or emotional turmoil at home. Lack of positive social interaction opportunities and support from caregivers can lead to social isolation and difficulties in forming friendships. The adolescent may struggle to connect with peers and experience conflict or bullying in social settings.

Adolescents raised in dysfunctional environments may be at higher risk for developing mental health issues such as depression, anxiety, eating disorders, or substance abuse. They may lack healthy coping mechanisms for dealing with stress and emotional challenges.

Overall, the caregiver's role during early adolescence is crucial for promoting healthy development and preparing the adolescent for adulthood. Positive and supportive caregiving fosters resilience, self-confidence, and well-being, while dysfunction can have lasting negative effects on the adolescent's physical, emotional, and social development.

Journaling & Reflection

How did the caregiving you received during infancy (0-2 years) influence your emotional security and trust in others? Can you identify any specific moments or experiences that shaped this foundation? As it relates to the material we've just gone over, can you see any cause/effect or similarities in your own life? Are you able to relate to any of the effects provided in your own life?

_____

_____

_____

_____

_____

_____

_____

_____

_____

_____

_____

In what ways did your caregivers support or hinder your development between the ages of 2 and 6? How did their approach to boundaries, independence, and social skills impact your growth during this period? As it relates to the material we've just gone over, can you see any cause/effect or similarities in your own life? Are you able to relate to any of the effects provided in your own life?

_____

_____

_____

_____

_____

_____

_____

_____

_____

_____

Journaling & Reflection

Think about your experiences between the ages of 6 and 12. How did your caregivers support your academic and extracurricular activities? What impact did their guidance have on your sense of responsibility and independence? Remember this is looking at how *you* experienced something, how *you* felt, not worrying about the feelings or thoughts of anyone else.

During your teenage years (12-18), how did your caregivers balance providing emotional support and allowing you independence? Were your opinions respected? Were you heard and valued when you voiced how you felt? How did their involvement influence your identity formation and decision-making abilities?

Journaling & Reflection

Reflect on any dysfunctional parenting you may have experienced during these developmental stages, based on what you now understand *disfunction* to be, based on the materials provided. How did it affect your emotional, cognitive, and social development? Can you identify any lasting effects on your self-esteem or behavior?

_____
_____
_____
_____
_____
_____
_____
_____
_____
_____
_____
_____
_____

Identify any positive and nurturing aspects of caregiving you received throughout your childhood. How did these experiences contribute to your resilience, self-confidence, and overall well-being, if at all? Refer back to the previous section for examples of specific results you may recognize in your own life.

_____
_____
_____
_____
_____
_____
_____
_____
_____
_____
_____
_____

Journaling & Reflection

When you were growing up did you ever feel unsafe about feeling how you did? Were there ever any situations when you felt like you didn't fit in? How about feeling like you were pushed aside, or un-prioritized when you felt you should have been a higher priority? Do you remember feeling like you needed to achieve a certain level of success in order to be accepted?

Section 2:
The Impact of Nature & Nurture

Nature is determined first by the integrity of our brain. Some children are born healthy with no abnormalities. Others are born with congenital anomalies: structural abnormalities in the brain presented at birth, can lead to developmental issues and neurological impairments. Other factors could be pre-mature birth or brain injury caused by a traumatic birth. There are a variety of factors that can compromise the integrity of the brain. Then, there is genetics. Our genetics play a crucial role in determining our overall health. The influence of genetics on health is multifaceted, impacting susceptibility to certain diseases, individual responses to medications, and even predispositions to certain lifestyle factors. Think of it as the basic foundation of our physical and psychological preparedness to engage with the world.

Nurture is an equally important part of this equation. It refers to the environmental and experiential factors that influence an individual's development such as early attachment experiences including the quality of parenting, the level of emotional support, the presence of a stable and nurturing family structure, and the quality of early childhood experience including interactions with peers, educators, and the broader social environment. All these things contribute to the development of social skills, communication abilities, and emotional intelligence. Positive relationships can foster a sense of belonging and emotional well-being.

In the last decade, contemporary psychoanalysis and empirical research have expanded the literature on epigenetics and inherited trauma, investigating the ways in which trauma is transmitted from one generation to the next and held in our minds and bodies as our own. In studying the intergenerational transmission of trauma, clinicians investigate how our ancestor's unprocessed emotions, especially trauma, are passed down as what is known as an emotional inheritance, leaving a trace in our minds and in those of future generations.

The "nurture" aspect in the nature vs. nurture philosophy refers to the environmental and experiential factors that influence an individual's development. While "nature" represents the genetic and innate factors inherited from biological parents, "nurture" encompasses the external influences that shape a person's traits, behaviors, and overall development.

Here are 9 key components of the nurture perspective that impact a person's development.

1. Family Environment: The family environment, including the quality of parenting, the level of emotional support, and the presence of a stable and nurturing family structure, significantly impacts a person's development. Positive family experiences can contribute to emotional well-being and social skills.

2. Early Childhood Experiences: The early years of life play a crucial role in shaping personality, cognitive abilities, and social skills. Positive early experiences, such as a supportive and stimulating environment, can enhance cognitive development and emotional resilience.

3. Social Interactions and Relationships: Interactions with peers, educators, and the broader social environment contribute to the development of social skills, communication abilities, and emotional intelligence. Positive relationships can foster a sense of belonging and emotional well-being.

4. Education and Learning Opportunities: Educational experiences, both formal and informal, play a vital role in shaping a person's knowledge, skills, and cognitive abilities. Access to quality education and learning opportunities influences intellectual development.

5. Cultural and Societal Influences: Cultural and societal factors, including norms, values, and expectations, contribute to shaping an individual's beliefs, attitudes, and behaviors. Cultural context influences socialization and the development of identity.

6. Economic Factors: Socioeconomic conditions and access to resources can impact a person's opportunities and overall well-being. Economic stability or instability can influence educational attainment, career choices, and overall life satisfaction.

7. Life Events and Experiences: Significant life events, such as trauma, stress, or positive milestones, can have lasting effects on an individual's psychological well-being. Resilience and coping strategies are often shaped by experiences throughout life.

8. Media and Technology: Exposure to media, technology, and cultural influences through various channels can shape values, beliefs, and behaviors. Media plays a role in influencing societal norms and individual perspectives.

9. Environmental Factors: The physical environment, including exposure to toxins, pollution, and access to green spaces, can impact overall health and well-being.

Journaling & Reflection

Do you feel that you received the emotional support you needed in order to learn healthy social skills? What did that support look like? How did you receive this support and from who?

_____

_____

_____

_____

_____

_____

_____

_____

_____

_____

_____

_____

How were your interactions with your peers and educators?

_____

_____

_____

_____

_____

_____

_____

_____

_____

_____

_____

Journaling & Reflection

Do you feel like the things expected of you were reasonable or unrealistic? How so? In what ways?

_____
_____
_____
_____
_____
_____
_____
_____
_____
_____
_____
_____
_____

Do you have much exposure to media, technology, or societal influences? How do you feel that this affected you both positively and negatively?

_____
_____
_____
_____
_____
_____
_____
_____
_____
_____
_____
_____
_____

Section 3: Attachment Theory & Family Systems

Attachment Theory, developed by John Bowlby and later expanded upon by Mary Ainsworth, is a psychological framework that centers on the bonds formed between infants and their caregivers. It particularly emphasizes how these early relationships shape an individual's emotional and social development throughout life. These styles include secure attachment, anxious-ambivalent attachment, anxious-avoidant attachment, and disorganized attachment.

The quality of the caregiver's presence, responsiveness, and availability plays a crucial role in determining the child's attachment style. Attachment theory suggests that the attachment style established in infancy influences an individual's relationships, emotional regulation, and ability to cope with stress in adulthood. Whether we form secure or insecure attachments sets the stage for our development and significantly impacts our ability to navigate relationships as adults.

The quality of the attachments formed with primary caregivers depends on their capacity to regulate their nervous system and the environment they inhabit, said another way, the system they live inside of.

As you're discovering in this workbook, no man lives on an island. Individuals grow up within systems, not only their family system but also within societal structures. These systems encompass both explicit and implicit rules, along with consequences for disregarding them. Within these systems, we learn lessons about power dynamics, values, morality, and how to negotiate them. Moreover, we discern our place within these frameworks. It is not uncommon to grow up feeling unsafe within certain systems. As children, we absorb messages from the adults around us, shaping our perceptions of ourselves: whether we're deemed good or bad, smart or foolish. Children internalize these messages from family and other authority figures, developing intricate coping mechanisms to navigate within these systems.

Unhealthy family systems are characterized by dysfunctional patterns of behavior and communication that negatively affect the well-being of family members. Here are several examples of unhealthy family systems:

1. Authoritarian Family

- Characteristics: High demands, strict rules, and expectations with little warmth or responsiveness.
- Examples: Families that follow strict religious guidelines and impose them on other family members, or families of great wealth where members are groomed to inherit or take over a family business despite their disinterest.
- Impact: Can lead to rebellion or compliance out of fear, poor self-esteem, anxiety, and difficulty in decision-making.

2. Enmeshed Family

- Characteristics: Lack of boundaries, excessive emotional involvement, and dependency among family members.
- Examples: Such families may compensate for physically or mentally ill members or rely on family resources (e.g. wealth). Children are often treated as assets that serve the family structure.
- Impact: Individuals may struggle with autonomy, and identity development, and experience high levels of anxiety.

3. Overprotective Family

- Characteristics: Excessive control and protection, preventing children from making their own decisions or experiencing failure.
- Examples: Overprotectiveness may aim to preserve family wealth and keep children from bringing outsiders into the family system.
- Impact: Can hinder the development of independence, self-confidence, and problem-solving skills.

4. Martyr Family

- Characteristics: One family member sacrifices their own needs and desires excessively for the sake of the family, often with feelings of resentment.
- Examples: This may involve parents staying together for financial reasons or not pursuing their dreams due to loyalty to the family system.
- Impact: Can lead to guilt and dependence among other family members and unresolved resentment in the martyr.

5. Controlling Family

- Characteristics: One or more family members exert excessive control over others, dictating decisions and limiting autonomy.
- Examples: This is often seen in high-status families i.e. families of great wealth, and religious families where there is significant control over marriages, careers, and education.
- Impact: Can result in rebellion, low self-worth, and difficulties in developing personal autonomy.

6. Perfectionistic Family

- Characteristics: High, unrealistic expectations and an emphasis on success and flawlessness.
- Examples: This is often seen in military families, high-status families i.e. families of high academic achievement (a long line of doctors/lawyers – alumni of elite Ivy League schools), great wealth, and religious families where there is significant control over marriages, careers, and education.
- Impact: Creates pressure, anxiety, fear of failure, and low self-worth in case of unmet expectations.

7. Conflict-Avoidant Family

- Characteristics: Avoidance of conflict and expression of negative emotions, leading to unresolved issues. Examples: Often, the primary authority figure has a personality disorder, such as narcissism, making it difficult for other members to express their feelings.
- Impact: Suppressed emotions, passive-aggressive behaviors, and lack of problem-solving skills.

8. Addictive Family

- Characteristics: One or more family members have an addiction (e.g. alcohol, or drugs) that dominates family dynamics.
- Impact: Creates an environment of instability, enabling behaviors, and neglect of emotional and physical needs.

The remaining examples are typical subsets of the addictive family system

9. Permissive/Neglectful Family

- Characteristics: Lack of structure, rules, and guidance; may also involve emotional neglect.
- Examples: Neglect is a form of covert abuse, where children might feel privileged but actually suffer from a lack of discipline and care due to the caregiver's addictions or disabilities.
- Impact: Children may struggle with self-discipline, respecting boundaries, and feelings of insecurity.

10. Disengaged Family

- Characteristics: Emotional detachment, lack of communication, and minimal involvement in each other's lives.
- Examples: Authority figures might be workaholics or have unresolved trauma, leading to an avoidant attachment style.
- Impact: Family members may feel isolated, and unsupported, and develop issues with trust and intimacy.

11. Chaotic Family

- Characteristics: Unpredictable environment with inconsistent rules, roles, and routines.
- Examples: often associated with substance abuse or mental illness.
- Impact: Leads to confusion, insecurity, and difficulty in forming stable relationships and routines.

12. Abusive Family

- Characteristics: Presence of physical, emotional, sexual, or verbal abuse.
- Examples: often associated with substance abuse or mental illness.
- Impact: Severe emotional trauma, fear, low self-esteem, and long-term mental health issues.

13. Scapegoating Family

- Characteristics: One family member is unfairly blamed for the problems of the family.
- Example: Often associated with substance abuse or mental illness.
- Impact: The scapegoated individual may suffer from low self-esteem, depression, and a sense of injustice.

14. Role-Reversal Family

- Characteristics: Children take on adult responsibilities or emotional caregiving roles.
- Examples: Often due to parental incapacity caused by addiction or mental/physical illness.
- Impact: Can lead to premature adulthood, stress, and difficulty in forming a stable identity.

Now that we have reviewed the concept of attachment and unhealthy family systems let's look at abuse. What is considered abuse? Most people have no trouble identifying overt forms of abuse unless they have disassociated and have blocked the memories of it. However, one of the most difficult kinds of abuse to recover from is covert abuse because we don't even know that it happened. I am going to distinguish how the two forms of abuse present distinctly:

Overt Abuse

Definition: Overt abuse is explicit and easily identifiable. It involves direct, obvious, and often physical actions or verbal expressions of abuse.

Characteristics:
- Physical Violence: Hitting, slapping, punching, kicking, or any form of physical assault.
- Verbal Abuse: Shouting, name-calling, insulting, or making threats.
- Sexual Abuse: Forcing someone to engage in sexual activities against their will.
- Intimidation: Using gestures, body language, or direct threats to instill fear.
- Public Humiliation: Abusing or embarrassing someone in front of others.

Impact: Because overt abuse is visible and blatant, it often results in immediate and recognizable harm. Victims of overt abuse may have physical injuries and may also suffer from severe psychological trauma.

Covert Abuse

Definition: Covert abuse is subtle and hidden. It involves manipulative behaviors that are not immediately obvious and can be difficult to detect.

Characteristics:
- Gaslighting: Manipulating someone to make them doubt their own perceptions, memory, or sanity.
- Emotional Manipulation: Using guilt, shame, or fear to control another person's actions or feelings.
- Passive-Aggression: Indirectly expressing anger or resentment through sulking, procrastination, or deliberate inefficiency.
- Isolation: Gradually cutting off a person from friends, family, or other support systems.
- Financial Control: Restricting access to money or resources to exert power over someone.
- Undermining: Subtly diminishing someone's confidence or self-esteem through backhanded compliments or constant criticism.

Methods:
- Overt Abuse uses direct actions like hitting, shouting, or making threats.
- Covert Abuse uses indirect actions like gaslighting, emotional manipulation, and passive aggression.
- The psychological impact of overt abuse is often immediate and acute psychological and physical harm.
- The impact of covert abuse is usually gradual and cumulative psychological harm, leading to long-term emotional and mental health issues.
- The impact of covert abuse can be insidious and long-lasting. It often erodes the victim's self-esteem and psychological well-being over time. Since it is less visible, victims may struggle to recognize it or may not be believed when they seek help.

Understanding these differences is crucial for identifying and addressing all forms of abuse. Both overt and covert abuse are harmful and unacceptable, and recognizing the signs of each can help victims seek appropriate support and intervention.

Identifying not only the unique patterns of the family system you were raised in but also identifying the difference between overt and covert abuse is a critical step toward addressing and healing the dysfunction within yourself as a result of having been raised in an unhealthy family system. It is possible to heal and go beyond the limitations of our upbringing. One of the goals of this workbook is to help individuals identify dysfunctional patterns so that they can seek healing, overcome the limitations imposed by their past, and become liberated to grow into the person they want to be.

Healthy Family System

Next, let's take a deeper look at what a healthy family system looks like. In a healthy family system, the parental figures or caregivers demonstrate effective communication skills. They express their thoughts and feelings in age-appropriate, considerate ways, listen actively to other family members, and respond thoughtfully. They display respect for each other and respect the other's individuality, opinions, and boundaries, fostering a sense of value and acceptance. They provide emotional support, creating an environment where members feel safe to share their emotions and receive empathy and encouragement.

There is a clear understanding of each person's roles and responsibilities, which are appropriate to their age and abilities. Each member shares in the household management and has a feeling of ownership and contribution within their home and family environment.

One of the cornerstones of healthy family relationships is healthy boundaries. Relationships require boundaries. It is important to know where one begins and ends and to distinguish between one's own energy and that of others. Respect for oneself and one's own feelings and needs, as well as respect for the personal space and autonomy of fellow family members, is essential. Autonomy and independence are crucial in developing healthy interdependent family connections. When respect and boundaries are present, this allows for healthy and effective conflict resolution. Conflicts are addressed constructively through negotiation and compromise, without resorting to aggression or avoidance

Healthy families have coping mechanisms and strategies to deal with stress and adversity, such as problem-solving, seeking support, and maintaining a positive outlook. They are also flexible and adaptable, capable of adjusting to changes and challenges while maintaining stability and support for their members.

A healthy family has shared values, traditions, and goals that guide their actions and decisions, creating a sense of unity and purpose. They spend meaningful time together, engaging in activities that strengthen their bond and create positive memories.

Healthy families are supportive, they acknowledge and celebrate each other's achievements and strengths, fostering a positive and encouraging environment. They support the individual growth and development of each member, encouraging them to pursue their interests and goals.

Here are some examples of what a healthy family system looks like:

Clear Communication: Family members feel safe to openly express their thoughts, feelings, and needs. They listen to each other attentively and strive to understand each other even when they have differing perspectives. For example, instead of avoiding difficult conversations, they address conflicts constructively and seek resolutions together.

Here is an illustration:

Daughter to mother: "Mom, I am hurt that you didn't attend my dance recital. Your absence left me feeling unimportant."

Mother's response to daughter: "Thank you for sharing your feelings with me. I apologize that I didn't clearly explain to you that I was unable to get out of work early that day. My team was on a deadline. I guess I just didn't realize how much it meant to you for me to be there. I promise, going forward, I will communicate more clearly with you so that there is no misunderstanding and please know that I would have been there if I could have. Supporting you is especially important to me. I love you very much and am so proud of your talents and abilities."

Emotional Support: Family members provide each other with comfort, encouragement, and validation. They offer empathy and understanding during challenging times and celebrate each other's achievements. For instance, they express love and appreciation through both words and actions, creating a nurturing environment where everyone feels valued.

Example: Son to Father:

Son – "Dad, Jane told me I was ugly. She laughed when I asked her to the prom. What if she's right?! What if I am ugly, I will never have a girlfriend."

Father – "Son, thank you for sharing your feelings with me. That sounds so painful. I am so sorry that she spoke to you like that. Sometimes people say mean things. That doesn't mean that they are true. This is an opportunity for you to trust your innate worth and not outsource your self-esteem to a teenager who is probably struggling with her own self-esteem. When you know your own worth, no one can ever take that from you."

Boundaries and Respect: Healthy families respect each other's boundaries and individual autonomy. They recognize and honor each member's unique preferences, interests, and personal space. For example, they avoid intrusive behaviors and seek consent before making decisions that affect others.

Example: When the family is together selecting a movie, podcast, or group activity, they consider the preferences of all participants and take mutual likes into account when making a choice. For instance, even if 4 out of 5 siblings enjoy horror movies, if the 5th sibling doesn't, the family chooses a movie that everyone can enjoy and the one sibling who doesn't like horror movies doesn't get shamed because he is less tolerant of violence than the others.

United Values and Goals: Healthy parents share common values and goals that guide their interactions and decision-making. They work collaboratively towards common objectives while also supporting each other's personal aspirations. They don't only spend time caring for their children, they make time to nurture each other and their relationship. For instance, they may prioritize spending quality time together and engaging in shared activities that promote bonding and unity.

Example: A healthy parental system abides by the same standards and ideals and teaches those things to their children not only by instruction but also by example.

Adaptability and Flexibility: Healthy families demonstrate resilience and adaptability in the face of challenges or changes. They are open to new ideas and strategies for problem-solving, allowing for growth and development as a unit.

For example, they adjust their routines or roles as needed to accommodate evolving circumstances, fostering a sense of adaptability and resourcefulness.

Healthy Conflict Resolution: Family members handle conflicts constructively, seeking mutually beneficial solutions without resorting to aggression or hostility. They practice active listening, empathy, and compromise to resolve disagreements peacefully.

For example, they may use "I" statements to express their feelings and needs while avoiding blame or criticism.

Overall, a healthy family system promotes emotional well-being, resilience, and mutual support among its members. It provides a nurturing environment where individuals can thrive and develop strong, fulfilling relationships with one another.

Your earliest experiences with caregivers, particularly how they provide affection and discipline, leaves a lasting imprint on an individual's personality, behavior, and emotional development. This concept integrates elements of attachment theory and behavioral psychology, suggesting that the patterns of love and punishment experienced during formative years create enduring templates for relationships and self-regulation.

Journaling & Reflection

Which, if any, of the unhealthy family systems can you identify with? Please be honest regarding your answers here. Remember this is how you felt, not how others believed you should feel, or how they felt.

_____
_____
_____
_____
_____
_____
_____
_____
_____
_____
_____
_____

Have you experiences either covert or overt abuse? In what ways and from whom?

_____
_____
_____
_____
_____
_____
_____
_____
_____
_____
_____
_____

Journaling & Reflection

How do you remember conflict being handled and/or resolved?

Section 4: Love & Punishment (Imprinting)

The way a child is loved, including the consistency, warmth, and responsiveness of caregivers, plays a crucial role in forming secure or insecure attachments. Secure attachment, resulting from consistent and loving care, leads to a positive self-image and healthy relationships. Insecure attachment, stemming from inconsistent or neglectful care, can result in anxiety, avoidance, or ambivalence in relationships. Early experiences of love teach children how to regulate their emotions. Caregivers who provide a safe and nurturing environment help children develop resilience and effective coping strategies. Conversely, lack of love or affection can lead to difficulties in managing emotions and increased susceptibility to stress. The way a child is loved impacts their self-esteem and sense of identity. Positive reinforcement, encouragement, and unconditional love foster a strong sense of self-worth. In contrast, conditional love or emotional neglect can lead to feelings of inadequacy and low self-esteem.

Punishment and Imprinting

How a child is punished shapes their understanding of right and wrong and influences their behavior. Constructive discipline that includes clear communication, consistent rules, and appropriate consequences teaches children self-discipline and accountability. Harsh or inconsistent punishment can lead to fear, resentment, and behavioral problems. The nature of punishment affects a child's relationship with authority figures. Having fair and consistent consequences for actions vs. harsh punishment helps children learn to trust and respect authority. Unpredictable or overly punitive discipline can breed distrust and defiance.

Children learn how to handle conflicts based on how they are punished. Positive discipline strategies, such as problem-solving and negotiation, teach children effective conflict-resolution skills. Punitive measures that involve physical or emotional harm can lead to aggressive or avoidant behaviors.

Long-Term Impact

Early imprints of love and punishment influence how individuals form and maintain relationships. Those who experienced consistent love and fair punishment are more likely to have healthy, balanced relationships. Individuals who faced neglect, harsh punishment, or inconsistent care may struggle with intimacy, trust, and communication. The early imprints of love and punishment shape an individual's self-perception and worldview. Positive experiences foster a sense of security and optimism, while negative experiences can lead to anxiety, pessimism, and a heightened sensitivity to rejection and criticism. Early patterns of love and punishment create templates for emotional and behavioral regulation. Children who receive supportive love and constructive discipline develop adaptive coping mechanisms and emotional stability. Conversely, those who experience neglect or harsh punishment may exhibit emotional dysregulation and maladaptive behaviors.

Understanding the impact of early experiences of love and punishment on imprinting highlights the influence of the ways we were parented and the caregiving practices employed. If we did not receive consistent love, clear boundaries, or constructive discipline, it is possible that we developed insecure attachments, leading to dysfunctional relational patterns. Fortunately, we live in a time where extensive interventions and therapies are available to address early imprints and help individuals overcome negative patterns, building healthier relationships and self-perceptions.

Journaling & Reflection

When you were disciplined, how long did it take for things to return to normalcy?

_____

_____

_____

_____

_____

_____

_____

_____

_____

_____

_____

Did your caregivers hold onto their anger for an extended period of time?

_____

_____

_____

_____

_____

_____

_____

_____

_____

_____

_____

Journaling & Reflection

Do you ever find yourself struggling to let go of the feeling of being wronged or treated unjustly?

_____

_____

_____

_____

_____

_____

_____

_____

_____

_____

_____

_____

If you have children of your own, do you ever find yourself punishing them for longer than appropriate?

_____

_____

_____

_____

_____

_____

_____

_____

_____

_____

_____

_____

Section 5:
The Masks We Wear (Maladaptive Coping Mechanisms As A Survival Strategy

Who are you?

We rarely ask ourselves this question. Perhaps we consider it during a job interview when a prospective employer asks us to tell them about ourselves, or on a date when the person across from us poses the same question. When asked, what do we say? Perhaps we identify with our profession or experience. Maybe we talk about our upbringing, the city we're from, or where we graduated. In a job interview, we might focus on our achievements and accomplishments. We might even share these details on a date.

Human beings often identify themselves by their histories, status, accomplishments, economic status, etc. Very rarely do we go beyond the surface to look deeper.

We might also identify with our general temperament, whether we are helpful and positive or lean towards being dark, depressive, or pessimistic.

Either way, we often see ourselves as fixed, immutable objects with particular traits or characteristics, as if they were assigned to us with no option to be different. We have all heard someone say, *"That's just the way I am."* If that were true, then transformation wouldn't be possible. Is it just luck that one person is able to escape the chains of addiction or the suffering of a depressive temperament while someone else remains the way they are forever?

How did we end up being who we are?

In the previous sections, we delved into nature, nurture, attachment, and imprinting. All of these experiences and imprints impact our decisions about who we become. At the moment when we are deciding, we often don't realize that a decision is being made. Typically, the decision is rooted in a reaction that occurs in a moment of needing to survive an experience that is scary or overwhelming. Let's explore the masks that we create to survive our upbringings.

The Hero

Do you consider yourself a high achiever who has always strived for perfection and often found yourself in leadership roles or caregiving responsibilities? If so, you might look back to your childhood. Perhaps you were considered mature for your age, the responsible one. Were you (and perhaps you still are) the go-to person in your family who provided leadership, guidance, and assistance to other family members? Perhaps you provided care to a sick parent or helped raise your sibling(s)? The "Hero" survived their upbringing by being indispensable, by being the person who maintained the family's image of success and stability and provided support and guidance to others.

The Black Sheep

Do you consider yourself unconventional, even a tad rebellious? Are you someone who has always stood out in a crowd and marched to the beat of your own drum? Perhaps you are an artist, a serial entrepreneur, a risk-taker, someone who thinks outside the box, and who may have struggled in school, disliked authority, acted out as a kid, or even had a brush with the law or a stint in rehab? You survived your family system by rejecting it. Taking the blame for your family's challenges or misfortunes as "Black Sheep" distracts attention from underlying family issues and expresses their dissatisfaction with the dysfunction within the family system by rejecting it.

The Invisible One

Do you consider yourself serious, studious, and focused? Are you the one who excelled in school behind the scenes (straight A's) but did not participate in extracurricular activities? Perhaps you are a writer, painter, or cinephile. You are the quiet, withdrawn type who hates attention and avoids conflict at all costs. One who seeks refuge in solitude or fantasy.

You survived your family system by minimizing disruptions in it by staying out of the spotlight, often overlooked or forgotten by other family members.

The Comedian/Entertainer

Do you consider yourself the life of the party? Are you someone who always has a great one-liner, who can hold the attention of any room, and find humor in any situation? Did you seek attention in school by playing pranks, cracking jokes, and getting in trouble for talking too much? Do you use humor or charm to diffuse tension and lighten the mood? Or perhaps you took on music or acting and found salvation in the spotlight? You survived your family system by minimizing situations and circumstances or providing entertainment that made them seem less painful. You provided comic relief and or entertainment to distract from family stressors while masking underlying feelings of fear or insecurity.

The Enabler/Co-dependent

Do you consider yourself a nurturer? Are you self-sacrificing, someone who can deal with anything that comes their way? Do you have an impressive capacity to deal with other people's insanity, bringing order to chaos? Are you considered the caregiver in your family who enabled the dysfunctional behaviors and even addictions or other family members, preventing other family members from experiencing the consequences of their actions? You survived your family system by maintaining the status quo by shielding other family members from facing reality or taking responsibility.

Peacemaker

Were you on the debate team in high school? Perhaps you went to law school. You are considered a great communicator, a diplomat, one who takes on the challenges of a conflict-averse family member who attempts to resolve disputes and maintain harmony within the family. You are the person that the elders come to when a matter needs to be negotiated between other family members. If your siblings are in a fight, it's up to you to save the day. Are your dad and uncle at odds again? No problem, you will be called in to turn things around. You survived your family system by acting as a buffer between conflicting family members, attempting to mitigate tension and promote reconciliation.

The Controller

Are you considered domineering or controlling? Perhaps you took on being a fighter or sought a career in law enforcement for all the wrong reasons. Maybe you became a dirty lawyer or a crooked politician. You are most comfortable when imposing rules, setting boundaries, and even resorting to abusive behavior to maintain power and control? You survived your family system by becoming a bully. You are perhaps a victim of violent abuse who was bullied yourself. Or perhaps you were entitled and spoiled. Either way, you decided to become bigger and badder to survive your circumstances and often used manipulation or coercion to maintain dominance. You may have also struggled with substance abuse issues and or may have a mental health diagnosis/personality disorder.

You may strongly identify with one of the above descriptions, or you may find yourself a mosaic, having traits from several of them. Regardless, we often find ourselves most comfortable in one character over another.

Journaling & Reflection

Were you able to identify with any of the masks or roles discussed? If so, which one? Or do you see more than one that resonates with you?

Section 6:
Healing Models & Modalities

In childhood, we were smaller, reactive, and trying our best to survive. We may have perfected these personality traits to continue surviving into adulthood. The good news is, we are not children anymore. We are not stuck with any of these characteristics. No matter who you decided to be in that moment, consider it was a decision made under circumstances of distress. Although you may have spent a lifetime perfecting that character, if any of those traits no longer serve the new vision of who you want to be, then you can move beyond those automatic ways of being.

You see, the characters we built in childhood were typically based on a foundation of fear and driven by our ego. The beauty of stepping onto a healing journey is that it allows us to transform. We can identify what no longer serves us and create a new character based on choice, not reaction, in service of our goals, not survival, steeped in a foundation of principles.

We are blessed to live in a time that has more information available to us than ever before. Thanks to modern technology and the integration of New Age psychology and transformational concepts into Western culture there is a greater emphasis on holistic health, mindfulness, and self-improvement. The blending of psychological and spiritual growth continues to influence contemporary approaches to mental health and personal development.

Socrates, a classical Greek philosopher, is one of the foundational figures in Western philosophy. He spent his life questioning the nature of knowledge, ethics, and the human condition.

The Socratic method, or Socratic inquiry, is a form of cooperative dialogue used to stimulate critical thinking and illuminate ideas. It involves asking and answering questions to stimulate critical thinking and to draw out underlying presumptions.

The phrase *"the unexamined life is not worth living"* is attributed to Socrates. This encapsulates the idea that self-examination and the quest for truth and virtue are essential for a meaningful life.

According to Socrates, an examined life involves:
- Self-Reflection: regularly scrutinizing one's beliefs, actions, and motivations to ensure they are just and true.
- Moral Integrity: striving to live a life consistent with one's ethical beliefs and understanding of virtue.
- Intellectual Humility: recognizing one's own ignorance and being open to continual learning and improvement.

As we are considering models for transformation let's look at one of the most powerful and effective movements of the 20th century.

The 12-step movement, popularized by organizations such as Alcoholics Anonymous (AA) and Narcotics Anonymous (NA), is effective at helping people transform their lives for several reasons:

Just like Socrates taught in 470 BC in Athens, central to the 12-step approach is the process of self-reflection, introspection, and personal growth. Participants are taught how to examine their thoughts, feelings, and behaviors, to identify patterns of behavior that are the source of their suffering and failure, and provide a structured program to help them change those patterns.

The 12-step program emphasizes that recovery is an ongoing process of learning, growth, and self-improvement. Individuals are shown how to work the steps, and they are encouraged to continue attending meetings throughout all stages of their recovery as well as guide others on their recovery journey, even after they have achieved sobriety and stability serving as a role model and support.

One of the key elements of the 12-step approach is the sense of community and support it provides. Individuals struggling with addiction or other issues can connect with others who understand their experiences, share their struggles, and offer encouragement and guidance.

Peer Accountability is a cornerstone of the 12-step model, individuals are encouraged to take responsibility for their actions and behaviors. Having a sponsor or mentor who guides them through the steps provides a level of accountability and helps individuals stay committed to their recovery journey.

The 12-step approach incorporates spiritual principles and encourages individuals to develop a connection with a higher power. This spiritual aspect provides a sense of purpose, meaning, and hope, which is a powerful catalyst for transformation.

The 12-step program provides a structured framework for recovery, with specific steps and guidelines to follow. This structure helps individuals break down their recovery journey into manageable steps and provides a roadmap for progress.

Accessibility and Availability: The 12-step program is widely accessible, with meetings held in communities around the world available at no cost both in person and on Zoom. This accessibility makes it easier for individuals to access support and resources when they need it.

Overall, the effectiveness of the 12-step movement lies in its holistic approach to recovery, addressing not only the physical aspects of addiction but also the emotional, spiritual, and social aspects. By providing a supportive community, structured program, and tools for personal growth, the 12-step movement helps individuals transform their lives and achieve long-term recovery.

If you are struggling with an addiction, such as alcohol, drugs, sex, gambling, codependency, love and sex, or food (eating disorders such as anorexia or bulimia), in addition to seeking professional treatment, adding the support of a 12-step program to your treatment plan can be a significant aid to your healing journey. It will complement the healing and recovery work you are doing with a professional clinician or treatment team.

Speaking of professional clinicians and treatment teams, how does therapy work?

Therapy works by providing individuals with a safe and confidential space to explore their thoughts, feelings, and behaviors, with the guidance and support of a trained therapist. Through various therapeutic techniques and interventions, therapy aims to help individuals gain insight into their challenges, develop coping strategies, and make positive changes in their lives.

One-on-one therapy involves sessions between a therapist and a single client. In this format, the therapist can focus entirely on the individual's unique needs, concerns, and goals. One-on-one therapy allows for deep exploration of personal issues and provides a supportive environment for personal growth and self-discovery. It can be particularly beneficial for individuals who prefer privacy, have specific concerns they want to address or feel uncomfortable sharing in a group setting.

Group therapy involves sessions with a therapist and multiple clients who share similar concerns or issues. In group therapy, individuals have the opportunity to interact with others facing similar challenges, share experiences, offer support, and receive feedback from peers. Group therapy can provide a sense of belonging, reduce feelings of isolation, and offer diverse perspectives on shared issues. It also allows individuals to practice social skills, improve communication, and learn from other's experiences.

A hybrid approach is often the most effective and is the approach used in most treatment facilities. In this format one has both a personal therapist in addition to participating in a group, alternating between the two formats and integrating them into a comprehensive treatment plan. The hybrid approach offers the benefits of personalized support and individualized attention from one-on-one therapy, combined with opportunities for peer support, social connection, and learning from others in group therapy.

The hybrid approach can be particularly effective for individuals with complex or multifaceted issues who may benefit from both individualized support and group interaction. It allows individuals to receive personalized attention and guidance from a therapist while also benefiting from the support, validation, and feedback of peers. Additionally, the hybrid approach can offer a sense of balance, flexibility, and versatility in addressing a wide range of therapeutic needs and preferences.

Whether in one-on-one, group, or hybrid therapy, the key to success lies in the commitment to personal growth, the willingness to actively engage in the therapeutic process, and the integrity of the therapeutic relationship.

Let's look at the Coaching Model and the fundamental difference between coaching and therapy.

Therapy is an experiential process that is open-ended, and typically focuses on healing, resolving psychological issues, and improving mental health. It addresses past traumas, emotional wounds, and underlying psychological patterns that may be causing distress. Coaching, on the other hand, is results-focused with an emphasis on personal or professional development, achievement, and enhancing performance. It emphasizes forward-thinking, building skills, and creating action plans to achieve outcomes.

In therapy, the primary goal is to promote healing, increase self-awareness, and foster emotional well-being. Therapists work with clients to explore deep-rooted issues, gain insight into their thoughts and behaviors, and develop coping strategies for managing challenges.

In coaching, the primary goal is to achieve specific outcomes and facilitate growth, success, and fulfillment in various aspects of life. Coaches help clients clarify their goals, identify obstacles, and create strategies to overcome them. The focus is on empowering clients to achieve their aspirations and maximize their potential.

Methodologies

Therapy typically employs a range of therapeutic techniques, such as psychoanalysis, cognitive-behavioral therapy (CBT), mindfulness-based approaches, and psychodynamic therapy. Therapists create a safe and supportive environment for clients to explore their inner experiences, process emotions, and work through psychological challenges.

Coaching utilizes a variety of tools and methodologies, including goal setting, action planning, accountability, and motivational techniques. Coaches may incorporate assessments, exercises, and constructive feedback to help clients identify strengths, overcome barriers, and take concrete steps toward their objectives.

Therapy often delves into deep-seated emotional issues, unresolved trauma, and complex psychological dynamics. It may address a wide range of mental health concerns, including depression, anxiety, trauma, addiction, and relationship issues. Coaching typically focuses on specific areas of personal or professional development, such as career advancement, leadership skills, relationship enhancement, time management, or lifestyle changes. It is generally more focused and results-oriented than therapy.

While therapy and coaching have distinct purposes and approaches, there can be some overlap between the two, especially in areas such as life coaching or executive coaching, where personal growth and development intersect with mental well-being. Once a certain level of stability has been attained in therapy adding a coach can help an individual take their lives to the next level.

Journaling & Reflection

Do you feel that the discussions within this workbook are going to be beneficial to your mental health? Remember, when I speak about mental health, I'm referring to how you view yourself and the world around you.

Section 7:
Essential Characteristics For Healing

Awareness: The first step of any healing journey is awareness. If I do not recognize the need for change and understand the seriousness of the current situation or problem, then no change can occur. However, one must develop the courage to become aware. It takes a courageous person to admit their difficulties and allow the awareness of truth to sink into their consciousness.

Motivation: The second step is a desire to change, often driven by factors such as personal values, goals, or external pressures. Pain and consequences are powerful motivators but the most powerful motivator of all is hitting bottom. If the pursuit of worldly things has left you bankrupt spiritually and or materially, perhaps you are now open to inspiration, and willing to turn your heart toward truth and allow yourself to fall in love with it.

Commitment: A firm decision followed by a willingness to act, despite potential challenges or setbacks. This requires dedication, to devote oneself to their healing journey.

Action: Checking into rehab, hiring a therapist/coach/or treatment team. In other words, you have taken concrete steps to implement change, including acquiring new skills, adopting different behaviors, or altering attitudes and beliefs. This requires integrity.

Persistence: Continuing to pursue change over time, even when faced with obstacles or resistance, and maintaining focus on the desired outcome. This requires the ability to put your ego aside and self-reflect without judgment. You can receive constructive feedback and even give it to yourself without allowing it to diminish you.

An honest self-assessment involves objectively evaluating one's strengths, weaknesses, behaviors, and beliefs without judgment or harsh criticism. It entails acknowledging both positive and negative aspects of oneself and accepting them as part of the overall self-image. In an honest self-assessment, individuals strive to gain insight into their thoughts, feelings, and actions to identify areas for improvement and personal growth.

On the other hand, self-condemnation involves harshly criticizing oneself, focusing primarily on perceived flaws, mistakes, or shortcomings. It often involves negative self-talk, self-blame, and a tendency to magnify personal failures while minimizing successes. Self-condemnation can lead to feelings of shame, guilt, worthlessness, and inadequacy, and it may hinder personal development and self-esteem.

The key difference between an honest self-assessment and self-condemnation lies in the attitude and approach towards self-reflection. While an honest self-assessment involves a balanced and compassionate evaluation of oneself, self-condemnation is characterized by harsh self-criticism and a lack of self-compassion. Honest self-assessment promotes self-awareness, growth, and acceptance, while self-condemnation fosters negativity, self-doubt, and disempowerment.

Unfortunately, self cannot reveal self to self, so it takes work with a qualified professional to help us gain the ability to self-assess.

Here are examples of self-condemnation:

- You are so lazy and disorganized; you are always late! No one respects you.
- You're an inpatient grouch. People don't like you. You are so sensitive.
- You're an insecure little tramp. Always looking for another notch on your bedpost.
- You are so weak. You can't hack being alone so you are always surrounding yourself with fair-weather friends. You're a loser.

Here are examples of self-awareness/reflection without judgment. Notice how curiosity takes the place of judgment or self-condemnation:

- When I don't wake up on time I am rushed and make mistakes. Why do I hit snooze 10 times instead of just getting up?
- I notice that I lose my patience and act mean toward people when I am overstimulated or tired. I need to have better boundaries and not overextend myself.
- I notice when I am lonely, I seduce men which always leaves me feeling empty after. Why do I continue to do this? I will discuss this with my therapist and continue to work on letting this go.
- I notice my anxiety levels skyrocket when I am alone. Why am I so uncomfortable being with myself?

If change is so easy then why doesn't everyone do it? Said another way, why am I struggling to make changes?

Did you know that there are actual stages/considerations that lead up to change? In the Stages of Change Model, we learn that common stages/considerations are leading up to change.

Pre-Contemplation:

In this stage, individuals are not yet considering change. They may be unaware of the need for change or resistant to the idea of changing their behavior. Considerations are increasing awareness of the problem or issue, recognizing/dealing with the negative consequences of current behavior, and acknowledging the potential benefits of change when it is pointed out to them.

Contemplation:

In this stage, individuals are aware of the need for change but may struggle with ambivalence or uncertainty about taking action. They may weigh the pros and cons of changing and may be considering their options. Considerations are exploring personal motivations for change, clarifying goals and values, assessing readiness for change, and seeking/being open to information and support.

Preparation:

In this stage, individuals are committed to making a change and are actively planning and preparing to take action. They may set specific goals, develop strategies, and gather resources to support their efforts. Considerations are setting realistic and achievable goals, identifying potential barriers and obstacles, developing coping strategies, and building a support network.

Action:

In this stage, individuals are moving forward with the plans, strategies, and goals they've been outlining and researching, utilizing the coping strategies and support network that they've put into place when needed.

Maintenance:

In this stage, individuals had achieved milestones along the way to their set goals and are exhibiting healthy behaviors that they wish to maintain in order to continue improving, growing, and moving forward. It's important to understand that most goals we set for ourselves are marathons, not sprints, so maintenance of these new behaviors is imperative to our longterm success.

Relapse:

This stage, while one that we try to avoid and circumvent at all costs, is still very likely to occur on occasion. It's important to remember that returning to our past behaviors or way of life can be temporary and in no way means that we have failed. Instead, it's a matter of refocusing on the goals and desires we have for ourselves then taking the time needed to prepare and take action back on the right path.

It's important to note that change is a dynamic and nonlinear process, and individuals may move back and forth between stages as they navigate their journey of transformation. Additionally, external factors, such as mental health, social support, environmental influences, and life events, can impact the pace and direction of change.

Journaling & Reflection

Do you find yourself assessing or judging instead of objectively evaluating a situation?

_____
_____
_____
_____
_____
_____
_____
_____
_____
_____
_____

Are you a victim of self-condemnation?

_____
_____
_____
_____
_____
_____
_____
_____
_____
_____
_____

Section 8:
Healthy Relationships

Without caring feedback, we don't grow, and it's essential to be invested in each other. According to Dr. Faye Snyder's Causal Theory, we believe that everyone is *"born good"* and that behaviors are not inborn. If we have issues with others, we treat them with regard unless they're actively hurting us. We communicate our experiences so they have a chance to change. We avoid judging and blaming and instead offer feedback.

Though this approach can be challenging, it becomes easier over time and helps us grow. We use "I-messages" to express our feelings and thoughts, assuming that respectful feedback helps us all improve. We don't judge or reject others but assess them and make decisions in our best interest.

We don't end relationships abruptly or "ghost" people. Instead, we explain our reasons for leaving, giving the other person a chance to self-correct, this is how we regard people. It's then up to you to decide how many opportunities you allow someone to have, to change their behavior, before you honorably leave the relationship (this includes both platonic and romantic relationships). In Zen and the Causal Theory, this is called honorable leave-taking.

If someone is hurtful, we must make them aware of the experiences we have had with them. To enable someone's poor behavior is to disable them from being better. By maintaining the relationship, we are in a way endorsing their actions. This section of the workbook covers your rights and responsibilities in relationships, emphasizing the importance of assessing other's ethics. Even if we can't always meet this standard, striving for it makes us better people.

Skill 1: Choosing the right friends & partners

 In relationships we often tend to make decisions based on feelings, not logic. This can be misleading because we are seeking to fill a void for something we did not receive during our developmental stages. This can result in relationships where we see the other person as a flattering reflection of ourselves. If this is the case, when the honeymoon stage is over, all of those feelings we experienced are no longer around. So instead, what we want to look for is consistency in a person as well as behaviors and traits that are from their authentic self.

Interestingly, unhealthy adult romantic relationships often mimic the dynamics of our early childhood experiences:

- Childhood Stage: Bonding, merging, symbiosis (Honeymoon phase)
- Adulthood Stage: Co-dependent merging

- Childhood Stage: Independence, separation-individuation, "terrible twos"
- Adulthood Stage: Acting out family system from childhood

- Childhood Stage: Interdependence (Adolescence/Adulthood)
- Adulthood Stage: Falling in love all over again

Understanding these patterns can help us make more conscious choices in our relationships.

A Quick Character Assessment

Below is a comprehensive list of questions to work through when you're connecting with and pursuing a new relationship, whether personal, professional, or romantic. Many of these questions are variations of those originally compiled by Dr. Faye Snyder PysD.

- How do they treat waiters and waitresses?
- How do they interact with children?
- Have they had long-term relationships before?
- Why did their past relationships end?
- How did those relationships end?
- Are they prone to blaming others?
- Do they take responsibility for their actions?
- What role did they play in past conflicts?
- Do they acknowledge their choices and their impact on their life?
- How do they handle disagreements? Do they argue fairly?
- Do they take responsibility for their part in a disagreement after you've acknowledged yours?
- Do they continue to harp on your mistakes even after you've apologized?
- Do they communicate issues using "I messages" or by blaming?
- Are they judgmental or quick to advise and blame?
- Are they open to learning good relationship and parenting skills?
- Do they need to make you wrong to handle criticism?
- Do they overreact with feelings or feedback?
- Do they rush into merging too quickly?
- Are they interested in sex without commitment?
- How do they handle responsibility for birth control and preventing diseases?
- Do they avoid deep, intimate conversations?
- Are they honest?
- Are they generally self-reflective?
- Do they use feedback to improve themselves?
- Would they make a good partner in personal growth?
- Do they want to truly know you and be known by you?
- Are they clear about their boundaries?
- Do they address their issues with you promptly?

- Do they ask for things politely, using "Would you...?" or "Could you...?" or "Please..."?
- How do they view commitment?
- What are their thoughts on responsibility?
- How do they deal with pain?
- Can they express their feelings effectively?
- Do they express their feelings too frequently?
- Do their feelings guide their choices more than their ethics do?
- Would you feel the need to change them if you lived together?
- Do they confront the truth in their own pain?
- What are their views on birth control?
- How do they feel about abortion?
- Would they want to keep a fetus with deformities? Would you?
- How long do they think you should know someone before sleeping together? Before getting engaged? Before getting married?
- How do they feel about your religion?
- How do you feel about their religion?
- Are your key beliefs compatible with theirs?
- Do they do the right thing even when it's tough?
- Do they take action when it's needed?
- What do they think drives serial killers to kill?
- Are they in favor of punishment?
- What's their opinion on spanking?
- What's their opinion on therapy?
- What's their opinion on parenting classes?
- Do they enable destructive behavior?
- Are they invested in a productive career?
- Can they meet their financial responsibilities?
- Are they overly controlling?
- Are they both faithful and trusting?
- What are their parents like?
- How do they feel about their parents?

Guidelines for Dating Relationships

These guidelines are flexible and can be adapted based on age and relationship type. Originally designed for youth, they apply to any generation. The goal is to prevent rushing into relationships without fully knowing each other, thereby avoiding potential issues like unplanned pregnancies or costly divorces.

Here's a more conversational breakdown:

1. **Pre-Date:** The man should give the woman his phone number instead of asking for hers. This makes her feel safer and shows he's interested in a date.
2. **First Date:** Go for lunch. Drive separately and meet at the location. This is to see if you like each other. No touching on this date.
3. **Second Date:** Have dinner together. Ask some important questions to get to know each other better. Maybe visit a museum or watch a movie afterward. A respectful hand kiss is fine, but no other touching.
4. **Third Date:** Plan a longer daytime activity, like visiting a theme park or going skiing. Holding hands or a light arm around the shoulder is okay. A kiss on the cheek at the end of the date is appropriate.
5. **Fourth Date:** Another dinner and movie date, followed by coffee or dessert. If things go well, holding hands during the movie and a kiss on the mouth at the end of the date is fine.
6. **Fifth Date:** Discuss your feelings about each other and if you want to date exclusively. If you both agree and are ready to handle the consequences of sexual intimacy, you can start moving towards it. Before becoming sexually intimate, agree on how to handle potential pregnancies and get tested for STDs together.

These guidelines are meant to help you get to know each other deeply, creating a strong foundation before becoming too involved. Avoid treating dating as a conquest, as it can be harmful. Use these steps to build a meaningful connection.

Skill 2: How to Relate on a Deeper Level

Sexual intimacy has a deep emotional and biological component. Women's bodies are more vulnerable and designed to receive, while men's bodies are typically stronger and dominant. Women need to feel safe and courted before being intimate. This need for safety and courtship should lead to commitment, which is even more crucial in an age of communicable diseases.

When the honeymoon phase ends, relationships often hit what Dr. Faye Snyder calls the "sexistential dilemma," where early intimacy habits clash with new expectations. Men might expect sex, while women might withdraw, especially if they had insecure attachments in childhood. This creates a cycle of men feeling rejected and women feeling pressured, leading to a downward spiral in intimacy.

To break this cycle, both partners need to rise above their current mindset, addressing childhood issues and finding generosity and gratitude. Women need to understand their partner's feelings of rejection, and men need to avoid taking their partner for granted, possibly courting them throughout their relationship. Mature, self-composed men who show less neediness are more attractive to women, who appreciate vulnerability and deep self-awareness as strengths.

How to Process a Disagreement

John Bradshaw's Change Model:
1. Perception: *"When I see/hear you..."*
2. Feelings: *"...I feel (mad, sad, glad, scared)."*
3. Interpretation: *"My fantasy is..."* or *"I imagine/worry that..."*
4. Needs: *"What I'd like from you is..."* or *"I wish/hope that..."*
5. Contract: *"If we could agree to..."*

The Side-by-Side Model

In relationships, you are responsible for your own choices and their consequences. It's not your right to change others or manage their behaviors unless they directly hurt you. When hurt, give clear feedback about your feelings without trying to fix their weaknesses.

For children, your choices matter greatly. Staying with a partner who is abusive, adulterous, or addicted can harm the children more than leaving. It's crucial to address these issues seriously, sometimes by separating to protect the children's well-being.

Side-by-Side Action Response:
1. You hurt my feelings: Express it gently, e.g. *"Ouch"* or *"My feelings were hurt when..."*
2. You harm my life: Use the Change Model language.
3. You hurt me again: Repeat the Change Model language.
4. You fail to change: Decide to live with it or leave.
5. With children involved: If there's abuse, adultery, or addiction, leave and file for divorce and custody. Reunite only if the partner shows genuine remorse, takes responsibility, and makes amends.

Principles of a Healthy Relationship

- **Respect Individual Feelings and Histories**: Everyone has their own feelings and past experiences, and they are valid.
- **Take Responsibility**: Each person is accountable for their actions and reactions to their past.
- **Understand Personal Perspectives**: Recognize that each person is in their own experience and might not be aware of yours.
- **Treat Others Well**: You are responsible for how you treat others and how you allow others to treat you.
- **Avoid Personalizing Other's Actions**: Don't take other's words, actions, or choices personally.
- **Avoid Manipulation**: Other people aren't there to be your doormat.

- **Speak Truthfully:** Be honest as best as you can.
- **Act with Courage:** Live your life courageously and do the right thing, especially when it's hard.
- **Communicate Constructively:** Share your thoughts with loved ones in constructive ways.
- **Live Authentically:** Be your true self.
- **Avoid Power Trips:** Don't exert power over others.
- **Support and Encourage:** Help others follow their hearts and reach their potential.
- **View Life as a Journey:** Life is a series of problems to solve.
- **Trust the Process:** Let others live their lives and trust their process.
- **Honor the Spirit:** Respect others in all relationships unless they oppress someone.
- **Leave Unhealthy Situations:** After giving feedback and warnings, leave unhealthy situations.
- **Learn from Mistakes:** Treat losses and mistakes as learning opportunities.
- **Allow Others Their Pain:** Don't try to spare others from their pain; it's part of their growth.
- **Own Your Issues:** Expect others to own their issues only if you own yours.
- **Express Vulnerably:** Speak from a place of vulnerable feelings instead of criticism.
- **Give Understanding:** To receive understanding, offer it first.
- **Reflect on Results:** Use the outcomes of your actions to guide you. If you keep losing friends, introspect on your behavior and choices.
- **Seek Feedback:** Look for reflections from others to understand how you come across.
- **Express Authentic Emotions:** Don't be afraid to show genuine strong emotions.
- **Minimize Ego:** Don't let your ego dominate your interactions.

Relationship Skills (as outlined by Dr. Faye Snyder PsyD)

Starting Out
- **Check Your Ego:** Keep an open mind and stay humble.
- **Observe First:** Get a feel for the environment before speaking.
- **Learn by Doing:** Be ready for baptism-by-fire learning.
- **Start with Trust:** Begin relationships with faith, not suspicion.
- **Respect Communication:** Don't dominate conversations or try to look good.
- **Own Your Mistakes:** There is dignity in owning mistakes.
- **Stay Humble:** Be prepared to be corrected. A lot.

Resolving Issues
- **Address Immediate Conflicts:** Prioritize live issues in the room.
- **Disagree Respectfully:** Use the Change Model for subjective feelings and Mirroring for objective feedback.
- **Express Hurt Properly:** Use *"Ouch!"* templates like *"I feel... when you..."*
- **Apologize Properly:** Use *"Oops!"* templates like *"I'm sorry, what can I do to make it better?"*
- **Avoid Assumptions:** Check impressions of motives with phrases like *"Forgive me, but when you..."*
- **Focus on Your Part:** Use *"I feel... when you..."* statements instead of blaming.
- **Never Blame or Judge:** Keep feedback objective and constructive.
- **Give Advice Sparingly:** Only give advice when asked.
- **Seek and Use Feedback:** Use feedback to improve how you come across.

Standards and Values
- **Assess, Don't Judge:** Focus on behaviors that can change, not inborn character traits.
- **Don't Enable Bad Behavior:** Avoid being a co-conspirator.
- **Ask, Don't Demand:** Use polite requests like *"Would you...?"* or *"Could you...?"*
- **Keep Your Word:** If you need to break a promise, notify the person and explain why.
- **Act Ethically:** Avoid scapegoating and making choices based solely on feelings.
- **Live Openly:** Excessive privacy can indicate unhealthy secretiveness.

Lifestyle

- **Live Authentically:** Aim for openness and honesty in your life.
- **Choose Relationships Wisely:** Pick people who also practice good relationship skills.

Etiquette

- **Address Issues Promptly:** Don't terminate relationships in the middle of a conflict without proper dialogue.
- **Avoid Secrecy:** Strive for openness and truthfulness, as secrecy can hinder growth.

Goals and Guidelines

- **Handle Heated Moments:** Learn to represent yourself well during difficult interactions.
- **Value Correction:** Embrace corrections as opportunities for growth.

Length of Commitment

- **Learn at Your Own Pace:** Relationship skills can be learned quickly, but most take longer. Humility and a desire to learn help speed up the process.

Breaking Bad Habits

- **Unlearn Unhealthy Patterns:** Replace old coping mechanisms with healthy relationship skills.
- **Mirror and Reflect:** Use feedback from others to understand and improve your interactions.

The Rules

- **Leave Your Ego at the Door:** Leave your pride behind to accept feedback openly and become your true, authentic self. Defending yourself shows you're not ready to self-reflect, so be open to feedback and focus on the process, not just the content.

- **Learn These Traits:** It will be necessary to learn how to love and live in the truth. Surrender your ego and learn how to self-reflect without judgement.

- **Own and Share Air Time:** Value everyone's time. Speak up but also allow others their turn. Balance sharing and listening to learn effective relationship skills.

- **Be Authentic in Trying:** Initially, new skills may feel awkward or fake. Push through this discomfort to uncover your true self, hidden beneath old coping mechanisms. Over time, you'll become more genuine and lighter.

- **Do Not Judge, Should or Blame:** When we 'should' someone, we're teaching. Healthy people don't judge, blame, shame, or condemn others. If you feel the urge to do so, understand it's likely from your own unresolved childhood trauma. Instead, focus on the process, and if necessary, seek private therapy to work through deeper issues.

- **Do Not Give Advice:** Don't offer advice unless asked. Unsolicited advice can feel oppressive and put you in a superior position. If you must offer advice, ask if the person wants to hear it first. People need to live their own experiences and will seek guidance when ready.

The Tools & Concepts

- **Stage One and Stage Two:** As detailed by Dr. Faye Snyder PsyD; Issues are categorized into two stages. Stage One are outside issues, things that happened and you are struggling with knowing how to address. Stage Two are live issues in the room right now and should be addressed immediately to prevent toxicity.

- **Framing:** When you're unsure how to say something, especially in charged situations, frame it. Use phrases like, *"I want to frame what I'm about to say,"* or draw a square in the air. This signals to the listener that you're trying to communicate carefully, reducing the risk of misunderstanding.

The Skills

- **Polite Requests: Would You, Could You, Please:** Use a humble tone when asking anything of someone, especially your partner. Avoid giving orders or speaking authoritatively, as it can be inflammatory. If you encounter anger in response, reflect on your own tone and approach before assuming the problem lies solely with your partner. Start requests with *"Would you...?", "Could you...?", or "Please...",* and make gentle physical contact with eye contact to increase the likelihood of a positive response. Remember, anything done for you is a favor, not an obligation.

- **The Eye of the Needle:** Revenge is often a result of childhood injury and misdirected anger. It can feel cathartic to vent on someone who offends us, but this only provides temporary relief and doesn't heal the underlying pain. True healing comes from recognizing and addressing the root cause of our anger, often a challenging process akin to passing through the eye of a needle. By transitioning from aggression to vulnerability, we can break the cycle of hurt and begin genuine healing, which is often accompanied by the release of long-held emotional pain.

- **Mirroring:** Mirroring provides objective feedback to help us self-reflect and correct our behavior. It involves reflecting back how others perceive us, often before an issue is fully presented or resolved. This process helps us recognize bad habits and become our best selves. Accept feedback without getting offended and use it to grow. Understand that disagreements and misunderstandings are opportunities for learning and developing empathy. Mirroring also helps us refine our outward persona, leading to more authentic and productive interactions.

- **Ethics in Confrontation:** Distinguish between giving unwanted advice and speaking out against immoral or unfair behavior. It's important to speak up when silence could harm others, but ensure your information is accurate and your intentions are constructive. Gossip is harmful, but sharing truthful and constructive information can contribute to a safe and honest environment. If you suspect someone is behaving unethically, address it carefully and verify the facts before taking further action.

- **Enabling:** Enablers avoid giving honest feedback to spare other's feelings, which can perpetuate unhealthy behavior. True kindness involves providing the necessary feedback for growth, even if it causes discomfort. Enablers may avoid confrontation due to their own fears, but this can lead to resentment and anger. In a workshop setting, enablers are encouraged to confront their fear of negative feelings and provide honest feedback to help others grow.

Styles of Communication

- **Yelling:** Yelling can make it difficult for others to hear you and may make you appear out of control. While there's no rule against yelling—since we don't support repression—it's generally better to start speaking softly and only raise your voice if needed. Some people respond to gentleness, while others need a firmer approach. Although yelling can sometimes be necessary to prevent an explosion of emotions later on, it's important to stay respectful. A healthy person can listen to someone yell without becoming defensive, as long as there's no name-calling, judging, or blaming. Occasionally, even a strong expletive can be a way of non-violently expressing frustration, but this should not be a regular occurrence in families, as it may indicate a need for professional help.

- **Feelings vs. Opinions:** People often confuse expressing their opinions with expressing their feelings, especially when using phrases like *"I feel that..."* which often disguises a thought or judgment. It's crucial to differentiate between thoughts and feelings for both self-awareness and effective communication. Instead of saying *"I feel that..."* try *"I think..."* or *"I'm having the thought that..."*.

- **Assessments vs. Judgments :** Judgments often involve writing someone off or making a final conclusion about their character, which can be harmful and mean-spirited. Judging can lead to retribution rather than healing, perpetuating negative cycles. In contrast, assessments are more scientific and focus on identifying behaviors and their origins, assuming they can be corrected or healed. Assessments help us make intelligent decisions without unnecessary emotional reactions. While value judgments are necessary for setting personal standards, they should not be confused with negative judgments.

Projections vs. Perceptions: Projections occur when we impose our beliefs about someone onto their identity, which can be harmful and crazy-making. Unlike perceptions, which are based on reality, projections feel real but are often not. It's important to distinguish between the two and seek reality checks to avoid harm. In workshops, we use The Change Model to address projections, focusing on expressing how someone's actions make us feel without accusing them. For example, *"When you ignore me at family gatherings, I feel unwanted, and I suspect you might not be happy to have me there."* This approach helps in addressing issues without projecting or judging.

Living with Honor and Courage

Myths to Dispel: Some people hold false beliefs like feeling entitled to their hypocritical views, thinking they can act without consequences, or believing they should follow strong feelings without considering the impact on others. They might think being true to oneself is the only priority in a relationship or that avoiding feelings is a valid way to handle internal conflicts.

Living with Honor and Courage: You're encouraged to live honorably and courageously by doing the right thing, even when it's tough. This often means confronting and processing old emotional wounds. Many people fear facing past traumas, but avoiding them only causes these issues to resurface in current relationships.

Keeping Our Word: How we keep our promises defines our identity. It's better to make fewer promises and keep them than to agree to something and not follow through. People who consistently break their word lose trust and respect. To deal with such behavior, maintain low expectations and minimal interaction until they change.

Right Actions, Wrong Consciousness: Some misuse relationship skills to avoid self-reflection or to assert superiority over others. Using skills to manipulate or to feel superior undermines their true purpose. Skills should be used for mutual understanding and growth, not for control.

Resolving Issues: Before ending a relationship, check if you are projecting or perceiving correctly. Communicate your concerns clearly and give the person three chances to address the issues. If you decide to end the relationship, do it respectfully and provide explanations to help the other person understand and grow.

Terminating Relationships: Your reputation is built on keeping your word and how you handle conflicts. The true character of a person is often revealed during the end of a relationship. Ending relationships with respect and clear communication is crucial. Avoid sudden departures or "ghosting" as it leaves the other person hurt and confused. Leaving prematurely means missing out on valuable learning and growth opportunities.

Journaling & Reflection

Did you read or hear anything in this section regarding relationships, as far as patterns of behavior or unhealthy habits, that you've displayed over time? What patterns, behaviors, and unhealthy habits do you see within your past relationships?

_____
_____
_____
_____
_____
_____
_____
_____
_____
_____
_____
_____
_____
_____
_____
_____
_____
_____
_____
_____
_____
_____
_____
_____
_____
_____
_____
_____

About the Author

Charles Shedrick, Certified Life Coach & Recovery Expert, is a heart-centered leader whose devotion to service inspired him to join the Army National Guard where he valiantly served for over a decade.

After the honorable completion of his military service, he began his civilian career in logistics. During this time he fell into what seemed like a harmless habit of relying on stimulants to boost his productivity, which led him down a dark road of addiction. After hitting bottom in 1999, he once again found himself in the Army, The Salvation Army, an organization with a mission to empower social justice and serve the community.

During his time there he was introduced to the 12-steps. Both of those organizations helped him discover that he needed healing both emotionally and spiritually. He gladly embraced all that he learned about himself as well as the guidance of those who had gone before him. He never looked back and has been sober ever since.

He was so excited about the treatment he received and his newfound sobriety that it was only natural for him to transition into treatment as a career. He knew from the bottom of his heart that his life mission from this point forward was going to be about helping those who suffered from substance abuse disorders to recover. He accepted a peer advocate position at his alumni program while simultaneously studying Addiction Studies at Glendale College completing as a specialist in Alcohol/Drug Studies.

The more he worked on himself and worked with others, he discovered that Sobriety was only the beginning. Soon this newly initiated spiritual seeker was expanding his horizons and seeking additional help and education.

He fortuitously came across a community foundation that provided counseling and coaching using a breakthrough methodology that hybridized complex psychological theories into layman's terms. The concepts were taught in both group and individual settings. He was expertly guided through that unique process that seamlessly allowed for the uncovering of unresolved childhood trauma. That experience connected him to feelings that he didn't know he had, feelings that had been pushing him around, imposing limitations upon him in ways that he had never before understood.

The therapists and staff provided him with a kind of unconditional regard that was familial in nature, which allowed for sufficient healing to take place, enabling him to connect with his authentic self, which was a first for him.

He fell in love with the theory and became certified in their modality. That was his first official coaching certification. The training, guidance, and work that he did during his time there as a facilitator and coach created the foundation for his career in mental health. He then went on to complete a second professional Life Coaching certification at The Life Coach Institute of Orange County.

Over the last twenty years, he has facilitated groups in various treatment centers all over Southern California. He leads specialized workshops on the basic text of Alcoholics Anonymous which is known as the "Big Book" which earned him the nickname "Big Book Charles." In addition to his workshops and groups, he is a gifted counselor and coach who works with individuals, couples, and families. His work is rooted in the values of self-awareness, honesty, and accountability. His fluency in the language of addiction, family systems, and trauma, along with the depth of knowledge gained from his own personal recovery journey make him an incredibly authentic, compassionate, intuitive, and insightful guide.

His life is dedicated to helping people understand why they do what they do - when they do what they do - providing them with alternative choices along with cutting-edge tools to help them break free from the chains of addiction and the complex family dysfunction that accompanies it, empowering them to discover their own untapped strength and infinite potential for freedom and recovery.

Charles continues to walk his talk by participating in his own recovery and spiritual evolution and continues to volunteer a portion of his time sharing the message.

For more information on how you too can work with Charles, visit his website - *www.charlesshedrickcoaching.com*

References & Additional Resources

Alcoholics anonymous big book (4th ed.). (2002). Alcoholics Anonymous World Services.

Bradshaw, J. (1992). Homecoming: Reclaiming and Championing Your Inner Child (p. 304). Bantam.

Snyder, F., Dr. (2012). The Manual: The Definitive Book on Parenting and the Causal Theory (p. 427). Clifton Legacy Publishing.

www.ingramcontent.com/pod-product-compliance
Lightning Source LLC
Chambersburg PA
CBHW042347030426
42335CB00031B/3484